BUILDING RELATIONSHIPS AT WORK

Self-coaching questions, inspiration, tips, and practical exercises for becoming an awesome manager

⌘

Managerial Competencies Series
Playbook No. 7

CÉLESTE GRIMARD

Copyright © 2018 Céleste Grimard, Canada

All rights reserved. All materials on these pages are copyrighted by Céleste Grimard. Reproduction, modification, storage of all or part of this book in a retrieval system or retransmission, in any form or by any means, electronic, mechanical, or otherwise is strictly prohibited without prior written permission from the author. Although every effort has been made to indicate the sources of text and ideas, it's possible that we missed some! If you're aware of references or citations that have not been provided, please contact the author. This book does not constitute legal advice and isn't a substitute for independent professional advice.

ISBN-13: 978-1979023504

CreateSpace, Charleston, SC USA

⌘
ACKNOWLEDGMENTS

I originally developed this series as a self-study, self-paced program for hundreds of managers working in a geographically dispersed area. Over the span of many years, these awesome managers offered me feedback, inspiration, and encouragement to transform this program into a series of practical, easy to read books accessible to all managers. Thank you! I also sincerely thank Rhiannon Ward for her assistance in editing and proofreading the books in this series.

CONTENTS

Series Introduction — 1

Introduction — 3

1. Reality Check: Self-Coaching Questions — 19

2. Inspiring Your Journey — 27

3. Tips for Awesome Managers — 33

4. Dilemmas: What Would You Do? — 69

5. Planning For Action — 74

About the Managerial Competencies Series — 77

References — 101

BUILDING RELATIONSHIPS AT WORK

Welcome to the Managerial Competencies Series!

The aim of this series is to help you understand and build the core competencies you need to become an awesome manager.

There's no getting around it. There are tons of journals, books, blogs, videos – you name it – on the topic of management. Yes, a lot has been written and said about how to be an effective manager. Everyone has their own spin to put on this topic, and research studies on this topic are practically endless. How does a busy manager sort through all the fads and

BUILDING RELATIONSHIPS AT WORK

fashions to find the nuggets of wisdom?

In designing this series, I pored over loads of resources and talked with hundreds of managers. I set aside all the fashions, fads, and fantasies, and I extracted only what is likely to be of enduring value to you. Although this series is geared towards practical, immediate use, I hope that it will provoke you to think deeply about managing and your role as a manager, and that it will make a difference for you so you can make a difference for others.

This module – Building Relationships at Work – is the seventh of 15 books, each covering a key competency of awesome managers. **Turn to page 77 to learn more about this series**, including the full slate of books, how each book is structured, and tips on how to get the most out of them.

Throughout the book, I refer to your **learning journal** and your **feedback team. These helpful tools are explained on pages 92 and 93.**

BUILDING RELATIONSHIPS AT WORK: INTRODUCTION

Awesome managers interact with others in a manner that demonstrates effective interpersonal skills.

BUILDING RELATIONSHIPS AT WORK

Effective interpersonal interactions are vital to managerial work. Most of a manager's day is spent communicating and interacting with employees, coworkers, clients, and others. Yes, you still need technical skills. But, the higher up the hierarchy you go, the more important interpersonal skills become. Many studies have demonstrated that, even if managers have technical competencies, not being able to work well with others results in perceptions of incompetence and eventual career derailment.

Communication is a process of give and take for which everyone shares responsibility. However, by virtue of their position, managers must take initiative and serve as positive examples in their interactions with others.

The communication process begins before an interaction occurs. Managers must establish trust and personal credibility by doing what they say they're going to do. Their communication effectiveness is proportional to the trust and respect others have in their integrity. They should avoid communicating

BUILDING RELATIONSHIPS AT WORK

when angry or irritated because this might lead them to say or do things that cause irreparable damage. Before interacting with others, managers need to develop a clear idea of what they intend to communicate and accomplish.

During the communication process, managers should strive to understand first and then be understood. Understanding means making time to listen and being a good listener. Being understood means using words that others will understand and an approach that is respectful of their own needs and those of others.

Effective interpersonal interactions involve a cluster of competencies:

1. Being aware of factors that influence communication
2. Listening interactively
3. Expressing oneself clearly
4. Providing and soliciting constructive feedback
5. Generating a positive impression of yourself

BEING AWARE OF FACTORS THAT INFLUENCE COMMUNICATION

Self-Concept

According to communication specialist, Myron Chartier, the foundation for interacting with others is a well-developed self-concept. How your see yourself affects how you see others and interpret situations. If you feel confident about your knowledge, skills, and abilities, you'll be able to talk with others about tough subjects such as turning down a request, receiving constructive feedback, admitting to a mistake, and voicing differing opinions. You won't feel threatened by people who hold different opinions, you won't feel that you know everything there is to know, and you won't devalue what others have to say. Indeed, all the competencies involved in personal mastery enable a person to interact with others in a mature, constructive, and productive manner.

Concentration and Filtering Challenges

Although most people talk in the range of 90 to 150 words per minute, we usually process over 300 words per minute. So, our ability to take in and deal with information far exceeds an individual's ability to present information verbally. This leaves lots of time when our brain is not actively listening.

As a result, we may be thinking about other things, thinking about what we're going to say, or even trying to develop answers to questions before they've been fully asked. In other words, we become inattentive to what the person is actually saying.

Listening Blocks

The listening process begins with hearing and paying attention to what someone is saying verbally and non-verbally. When these messages are interesting or important, we tend to pay attention to them. There are filters in

the "database" in our brains that attach personal meaning to information as it's presented; for example: previous experiences, expectations, values, biases, emotional hot buttons, knowledge, feelings, language and vocabulary. Our filters can also be based on:
- wanting to avoid difficult subjects
- hearing only what we expect or want to hear
- being overly reactive to certain words
- not liking the other person
- environmental distractions such as odors or sounds
- being distracted by a person's nonverbals such as their appearance, accent, tone of voice, or body movements

LISTENING INTERACTIVELY

People communicate content (what they're literally saying), meaning (what they intend to say), and feelings (their emotional state). The active listening process involves understanding a person's content, meaning, and feelings by paying attention to their words, tone of voice, and nonverbals. *Understanding* is demonstrated in the skills of reflecting, paraphrasing, and questioning. People don't feel like they have been heard unless there's an appropriate response to all aspects of their communication.

Words, Tone of Voice, and Nonverbal Cues

You're listening for content when you focus on words. This helps you organize the speaker's main points and the supporting points in a logical order. It allows you to better follow, remember, and respond to what the speaker is saying. A person's tone of voice and non-verbals provide additional information that reveals a speaker's underlying motivation. Most voices convey about 30% of the meaning of a message. Non-verbal cues, or body language, are messages sent by such things as a speaker's gestures, facial expressions, eyes, and posture. They confirm or deny what is said and how it's said. More than 50% of human interactions occurs through non-verbal communication. The table below contains some interpretations of common behaviors offered by image consultant, Victoria Seitz.

Nonverbal Behavior	Interpretation
Standing with hands on hips	Readiness, aggression
Arms crossed on chest	Defensiveness, closed
Hand to cheek	Evaluation, thinking
Touching nose	Doubt
Rubbing an eye	Doubt, disbelief
Rubbing hands	Anticipation
Pinching bridge of nose, eyes closed	Negative evaluation
Tapping fingers	Impatience
Steepling fingers	Authoritative
Tilted head, lean forward	Interest
Stroking chin	Trying to make a decision
Looking down, face turned away	Disbelief

BUILDING RELATIONSHIPS AT WORK

Listening for Content, Meaning, and Feelings

People feel better when you **acknowledge their feelings** as well as the facts. In reflecting feelings, you describe the other person's feelings in an empathetic manner, as you perceive them (without expressing approval or disapproval) to see if you have correctly understood how they feel. Here's an example, "I get the feeling that you're nervous in this interview. Is that right?"

We often assume that we understand what a person is saying without checking the accuracy of our perceptions. **Paraphrasing**, which involves restating the speaker's message in your own words, is a way of determining whether or not you correctly understood what they said. It significantly increases the accuracy of communication and, as a result, the degree of mutual understanding between yourself and the speaker. Two ways of beginning a paraphrase include, "Do you mean..." and "So, are you saying..."

Asking questions not only helps you to obtain clear and complete information, but it also lets others know that you're interested what they have to say. Use open-ended questions to encourage people to speak freely. Some examples include: "Can you tell me more about that?" or "How would you like things to be?" Use closed questions to request information that limits response options, often "yes" or "no" or a choice of a few alternatives. For example, "Did you bring your report?" or "Can you do this by Friday?"

EXPRESSING YOURSELF CLEARLY

Verbally, expressing yourself clearly involves saying what you mean in a way that's understandable to others. This requires thinking before you speak, organizing your thoughts, putting emphasis on key information, and checking for understanding. Nonverbally, expressing yourself clearly involves being aware of your tone of voice and your physical actions and reactions.

Appropriately Disclosing Oneself to Others

Self-disclosure means communicating your thoughts and feelings to others. Over-disclosers communicate way too much information at the wrong time. This can lead to embarrassment, confusion, time wasting and, sometimes, a loss of respect. Under-disclosers, on the other hand, communicate way too little information, perhaps out of fear that others will use the information against them, think less of them, accuse them of bragging, or discount their opinions.

According to business professors Ron Adler and Russell Towne, you might disclose something as a way of clarifying personal thoughts and feelings, inciting someone else to disclose information, creating a positive impression, and maintaining relationships. Self-disclosure is appropriate when the risk involved in disclosing is reasonable, it's likely to have a constructive effect, it's relevant to the situation, and it will likely be reciprocated. Keep in mind that you can't have a relationship with others without some amount of self-disclosure. By trying to keep yourself "hidden" or acting "mysterious," you distance yourself from others and lessen how much they trust you.

PROVIDING AND SOLICITING CONSTRUCTIVE FEEDBACK

Feedback is a way of "helping someone perceive their behaviors in the way that others see them." In almost every part of a manager's job – training, coaching, communicating, disciplining, and conducting performance reviews – feedback is necessary and, more often than not, a problem.

Managers may forget to give positive feedback to employees because they're busy, they think that employees already know that they're appreciated, or for some other reason.

BUILDING RELATIONSHIPS AT WORK

You should never underestimate the impact that showing appreciation – even for "little" things – can have on employees' morale and their motivation to contribute to the team.

Understandably, some managers are reluctant to provide negative feedback because they feel anxious about it or intimidated by an employee's potential reaction. However, when managers avoid giving needed feedback, an employee who is performing poorly doesn't find out about it. Time passes, and, finally, when you must deal with it, the employee is surprised, defensive, and resentful: "You never told me this before!" Moreover, not giving feedback when it's needed sets a poor example for others: "It's OK to be like that because Joe gets away with it," or "It's OK to be like that because the manager won't deal with it." The more you put off dealing with a situation, the more anxious you become, and the worse it is when you finally deal with the situation. It's a vicious cycle.

BUILDING RELATIONSHIPS AT WORK

Feedback is appropriate when:

1. There's a sufficient base of trust between you and the person. If they don't trust you, they will probably not accept the feedback, even if it's accurate.
2. Your intention is to help, and you believe you can help.
3. The person is important enough to you to make the effort to work out the issue, and you have the time to do so.
4. The person isn't feeling overwhelmed with other troubles (at work or at home).
5. The person isn't doing the best they can and is able to improve the situation.
6. The issues are likely to happen again and are within the person's control. If the incident is unlikely to repeat itself, weigh carefully what your motive really is. Also, if the other person isn't able to correct the situation to your liking, your feedback is likely to only make matters worse.
7. You have checked your perceptions with others first, and they have validated them.

8. You are willing to hear what the person has to say in their defense.

GENERATING A POSITIVE IMPRESSION OF YOURSELF

The reality in today's organizations is that it's not enough to "let your performance speak for itself." Is it a question of who you know rather than what you know? Depending on how political an organization is, being successful is usually a combination of being a high performer and a great person to work with.

It goes without saying that incompetent people who are a challenge to work with (i.e., people who are critical, irritable, defensive, and belittling of others) aren't desirable coworkers or managers. High performers who are also difficult to work with or who simply avoid interpersonal interactions don't tend to receive promotions, recognition, and appreciation either. And people who play the political game or "suck up" may be seen as excessively self-focused and self-serving. They're creating a false impression of themselves rather than building an impression based on who they really are. Sooner or later, "the jig will be up."

Ideally, you are a high performer and a people person. You recognize that you need to take the initiative to work with people and through people to be successful. You don't sacrifice your personal integrity in exchange for more influence. Rather, you try to influence by setting a positive example, developing excellent work skills and knowledge of your organization, and establishing and maintaining good relationships with everyone.

1

REALITY CHECK: SELF-COACHING QUESTIONS

To help you examine your relationship building and communication skills and challenges, we invite you to ask yourself a series of self-coaching questions. While thinking about your behavior in the past six months, find specific examples that support your answers. Consider whether or not "counter examples" exist; in other words, times when you may not have behaved in a manner that is consistent with your answer. In answering these questions, think about how you generally are rather than temporary aberrations due to stress or other factors.

Your answers to these self-coaching questions will shine a light on how you see yourself. If you know yourself well, your answers will be right on the mark. However, many people don't have accurate self-perceptions because they're not used to assessing themselves, they feel uncomfortable with the idea of reflecting on their own behaviors, or they truly don't know themselves well. As a result, their answers may be *extremely* inflated or low.

In all cases, but especially when answers are extreme (in any direction), seeking candid and honest feedback from others can be a valuable way of shedding light on your actual competency levels. You can learn a lot more about yourself if you get feedback from others.

BUILDING RELATIONSHIPS AT WORK

You can ask people to answer some of these self-coaching questions about you and provide examples or anecdotes of situations that illustrate their answers. They may not tell you what you want to hear, but it may be exactly what you need to help you make progress on your journey toward becoming an awesome manager. As American writer Herbert Sebastian Aga said in his book *A Time for Greatness*, "the truth that makes men free is, for the most part, the truth which men prefer not to hear."

Asking others for feedback takes courage on everyone's part. Others don't necessarily have the same picture of you as you have of yourself, and people are sometimes reluctant to "tell it like it is." However, "feedback-lite" that is polite and tells you what you hope to hear won't help you grow as a person. Tell people that you need the straight goods (politely though!).

BUILDING RELATIONSHIPS AT WORK

The Interpersonal Communication Inventory created by Millard Bienvenu and the Positive Impression Survey by Andrew DuBrin inspired some of the following questions.

→ Am I able to clearly express my thoughts and intentions? Or, is what I say easily and often misinterpreted?
→ Do I ensure that others have correctly understood what I'm saying? Or, do I simply presume that they understood?
→ Do I ask others for their feedback or reactions to what I'm saying? Or, do I avoid doing so (perhaps not wanting to hear their opinion)?
→ Is it easy for me to talk with others? Am I cordial and polite? Or, do I tend to avoid people altogether?
→ Do I talk about subjects that interest everyone? Or, do I focus on my favorite topics?
→ When what someone else is saying isn't clear, do I ask them to explain what they're

saying? Or, do I simply pretend to understand what they're saying?
→ Do I try to understand where the other person is coming from? Or, do I focus on my point of view?
→ Am I accepting of opinions that disagree with mine? Or, do I push my opinion on others?
→ Do I share talk time? Or, do I dominate it?
→ Do I contribute to conversations? Or do I passively allow the other person to dominate talk time?
→ Am I able to address issues or differences of opinions with others in a calm and reasonable manner? Or, do I get angry and defensive?
→ Am I willing to apologize for my errors? Or, do I feel that I never make errors?
→ Do I let people know when they have hurt my feelings? Or, do I avoid them, stew in my feelings, or talk to a third person about my hurt feelings?

BUILDING RELATIONSHIPS AT WORK

→ Do I smile and greet people when I see them? Or, do I expect them to greet me first?

→ Am I generous with compliments and quick to forgive? Or, do I rarely compliment others, and seek revenge for others' blunders?

→ Do I give others time to say what they have to say? Or, do I tend to interrupt them?

→ Do I listen actively and focus on what others are saying? Or, do I let my mind wander, prepare what I have to say, or judge what the person is saying?

→ Do I give immediate non-evaluative, specific feedback related to others' behaviors? Or, do I make judgements about their behaviors and intentions, and postpone giving feedback (if at any)?

→ Do I share credit with others? Or, do I tend to attribute successes to myself and failures to others?

BUILDING RELATIONSHIPS AT WORK

→ Do I look for common ground with others? Or, do I tend to focus on differences and things we don't have in common?

→ Do I tend to be cheerful, calm, diplomatic, and easy to be around? Or do I tend to be negative, stressed, demanding, or tactless?

→ Do I work well with others as a team player? Or, do I prefer to do things my own way without collaborating with others?

→ Do I do favors for others and extend a helping hand when I see that they need help? Or, do I avoid helping others altogether or unless they have first helped me (in a tit-for-tat fashion)?

→ Do I have a positive attitude and go out of my way to make others' day better? Or, do I feel discouraged and passively sit back waiting for "things to change around here"?

→ Am I a reliable, well organized high performer who follows through on my commitments? Or, am I an undependable, disorganized mediocre performer who promises but doesn't always deliver?

Reflection

What do your answers say about your perceptions of your relationship building strengths and opportunities for improvement? Do you consider yourself to be an effective communicator? Do you make a good impression? Do you give thoughtful and constructive feedback? Or do you feel like you could listen more attentively, express yourself more clearly, or give feedback more effectively? What feedback have others given you about your communication and relationship-building skills? How much overlap is there between your personal view and others' opinions? If they don't overlap well, why might this be the case?

Whether you think that you're an excellent relationship-builder or that you need to become a more effective communicator, the important thing is to use this reflection as an opportunity to make improvements.

2

INSPIRING YOUR JOURNEY

As you read through the following quotations, take note of the ones that speak to you the most. Then consider the message they are conveying to you.

BUILDING RELATIONSHIPS AT WORK

The most important thing in communication is to hear what isn't being said. - *Peter Drucker*

⌘

Kind words can be short and easy to speak, but their echoes are truly endless. - *Mother Teresa*

⌘

If you can talk with crowds and keep your virtue, or walk with kings – nor lose the common touch, if neither foes nor living friends can hurt you, if all men count with you, but none too much, yours is the Earth and everything that's in it. - *Rudyard Kipling*

⌘

You can't live a perfect day without doing something for someone who will never be able to repay you. - *John Wooden*

⌘

The art of conversation lies not only in saying the right thing at the right time, but in leaving unsaid the wrong thing at the tempting moment. - *John Charles Daly*

BUILDING RELATIONSHIPS AT WORK

Get into the habit of putting a kind interpretation on all you see and hear, and of having kind thoughts of everyone of whom you think. Never say behind a man's back what you are ashamed to say to his face.
- *Lawrence Lovasik*

⌘

I have striven not to laugh at human actions, not to weep at them, nor to hate them, but to understand them. - *Benedict Spinoza*

⌘

We should never pretend to know what we don't know, we should not feel ashamed to ask and learn from people below, and we should listen carefully to the views of the cadres at the lowest levels. Be a pupil before you become a teacher; learn from the cadres at the lower levels before you issue orders. - *Mao Tse-tung*

⌘

Always recognize that human individuals are ends, and do not use them as means to your end. - *Immanuel Kant*

BUILDING RELATIONSHIPS AT WORK

It is the province of knowledge to speak, and it is the privilege of wisdom to listen.
- *Oliver Wendell Holmes*

⌘

Nothing is sometimes the right thing to say.
- *Malcolm Forbes*

⌘

Oh, if the good spirit would only give us the power to see ourselves as others see us.
- *Robert Burns*

⌘

The easiest person to deceive is one's own self.
- *Edward Bulwer-Lytton*

⌘

Speech is the mirror of the soul; as a man speaks, so he is. - *Publilius Syrus*

⌘

The way we treat people poorly in organizations is mostly by acts of omission and noncommunication. - *Peter Block*

BUILDING RELATIONSHIPS AT WORK

If you want to make friends, go out of your way to do things for other people – things that require time, energy, unselfishness, and thoughtfulness. A kind word or a kind act is like lighting another man's candle with your own, which loses none of its brightness by what the other gains. - *Lawrence Lovasik*

⌘

People have an emotional bank account for each relationship; we make deposits when we are trusting, empathetic, and dependable. We make withdrawals when we are inconsiderate, dishonest, and arbitrary. When our accounts become overdrawn, we have to be especially careful about everything we say in case it is misinterpreted. It leads to defensiveness in which people are most concerned about defending themselves. - *Stephen Covey*

⌘

Letting people in is largely a matter of not expending energy to keep them out.
- *Hugh Prather*

BUILDING RELATIONSHIPS AT WORK

There are many different kinds of death, not all of them physical. There are murders as subtle as a turned eye. Dante was inspired to instill Satan in ice, cold indifference being so common a form of evil. - *Anne Truitt*

⌘

Wise men speak because they have something to say; fools because they have to say something. - *Plato*

⌘

The single biggest problem in communication is the illusion that it has taken place.
- *George Bernard Shaw*

What are your five favorite quotations?

Why do these stand out for you?

Which would you want to adopt as your personal motto? Include on the signature line of your emails? Post on your desk?

ns at Work

3
TIPS FOR AWESOME MANAGERS

As you review the following tips for building relationships, circle, check or highlight those that are especially meaningful for you.

BUILDING RELATIONSHIPS AT WORK

Listen effectively.

1. **Be attentive.** To do otherwise is disrespectful. Avoid reading, looking at your cell phone, or doing something else when someone is talking with you.

2. **Be patient.** People speak at different speeds and provide varying levels of detail. Allow others to finish what they have to say. You would want this treatment yourself, wouldn't you?

3. **Be open to what others have to say.** Try to understand the other person's position rather than preparing your rebuttal.

4. **Listen to what is being said** (the big picture) **and how it's being said** (the feelings, the intention). Also, pay attention to what is not being said. Sometimes, this can be quite informative.

BUILDING RELATIONSHIPS AT WORK

5. **When there are language barriers**:
   a. Be empathetic with others. Realize that they are doing their best, and that they are demonstrating courage by communicating in another language. Put yourself in their shoes.
   b. Be patient with yourself if you're having trouble communicating in another language. If possible, plan what you want to say ahead of time.

6. **Acknowledge distractions** when they exist, and try to address them directly (e.g., by going to a quiet place, by closing the door, etc.).

7. **After someone has spoken, ask others to restate what has just been said before they make their contribution.** This is especially helpful in team meetings where people may not be listening to what a speaker is saying. This is evident when their

comments don't refer to or build on what others have just said.

8. **Avoid the 12 blocks to listening** identified by Matthew McKay, Martha David, and Patrick Fanning in their popular book, *Messages: The Communication Skills Book:*
   a. **Comparing** yourself (your looks, your accomplishments, your success, you luck in life, etc.) to others. When you're busy comparing yourself to others while they're talking, you're not really listening.
   b. **Mind reading**, or making presumptions about what others are thinking or intending, rather than taking their words at face value. Mind reading also involves making assumptions about what others are thinking about you.
   c. **Rehearsing** what you're going to say once a person is done talking, instead of truly listening to what the person is saying.

d. **Filtering** out things that you don't want to hear such as criticisms or suggestions for improvement. Paying attention only to certain things that the person is saying, for example what is important to you and ignoring what is important to the speaker.

e. **Judging** the speaker and what they're saying, perhaps expecting the worst from them and, as a result, not truly listening to what they have to say.

f. **Dreaming** or thinking about something else, perhaps something that the person just said. When you're bored or anxious, you're more likely to engage in dreaming.

g. **Identifying** or relating what the person is saying to yourself. Before the person can finish their story, you might even start talking about your own experiences. Your focus is totally on yourself; you believe that your experiences are more important and interesting than those of the speaker.

h. **Advising**, or being quick to offer your suggestions and solutions even when they haven't been requested. As a result, the person doesn't feel like you have listened to what they're saying. This is a tempting listening block for managers who believe that their job is to solve problems. But, keep in mind that, sometimes, people just want to feel heard; they want someone to listen to them.

i. **Arguing**, or being quick to disagree, contest, and "pick apart" what the speaker is saying without giving them a chance to complete their thoughts. Sparring might involve sarcastic put-downs or discounting others.

j. **Being right** 100% of the time with little or no openness to others' points of view. As the authors suggest, if you suffer from this block, you'll do whatever is necessary to avoid "being wrong." As a result, diverging opinions, criticisms, or feedback are off limits.

k. **Derailing** the conversation by abruptly changing the topic or discounting what someone else is saying.

l. **Placating** the speaker as a way of appearing supportive, but not making an effort to really understand what the speaker is saying.

Pay attention to your nonverbal cues.

9. **Look directly** at the person and lean slightly forward. Nod your head occasionally (as appropriate) and offer verbal cues that you're listening such as *Oh*, *hmm*, and others.

10. **Use hand gestures and facial expressions that are consistent with your tone of voice and what you're saying.** For example, don't

say that you're open to what the other person is saying while crossing your arms.

11. **Pay attention to your tone of voice.** A firm and even tone conveys knowledge and experience. A warm voice tone conveys understanding.

12. **Smile!** It makes you more approachable.

Engage in positive interpersonal interactions.

13. **Show an active interest in others.** As communication expert Kristina Lanier suggests, instead of waiting for others to initiate a conversation with you, take the lead yourself. Talk to them about their favorite subject: themselves! Try asking open-ended questions that discourage yes/no answers such as "How did you get started in your career?" But, be careful to not interrogate the other person with 50 questions.

14. **Take advantage of free information that others offer.** If you listen carefully to what others say, they will probably leak free information: extra tidbits about themselves that you can use to keep the conversation going. For example, if you're talking about the weather, and the other person says that they may have to put their camping plans on hold, you can segue into inquiring about these plans.

15. **Do your share of the work in the conversation.** Don't expect others to show interest in you if you're not showing interest in them. Share information about yourself; extremely brief responses don't keep a conversation going. At the same time, don't monopolize the conversation. Keep it 50-50. When you're the one doing most of the talking, you're hogging talk time and coming across as self-centered. Also, don't monopolize a person's time. By talking only with you during a break, for

example, that person doesn't have the chance to talk with others. When you're in a group, and you draw a person's attention away from the group discussion by initiating a side conversation with them, that person misses out on the group discussion and may resent you for it.

16. **Engage in self-disclosure.** You need to risk "putting yourself out there" if you want your relationship to progress from stranger to trusted colleague or acquaintance to friend. In other words, you need to share personal information that helps others get to know you better so that they feel free to do so in return. This enhances feelings of intimacy but it could also make you feel more vulnerable. Moreover, it's easier for people to trust you when they know you. If you say nothing about yourself, people will "create" their own stories and ideas of who you are and what your motives are. Communication experts Steven Beebe,

BUILDING RELATIONSHIPS AT WORK

Susan Beebe, and Mark Redmond suggest that you test the waters gradually. When sharing personal things about yourself, start with non-sensitive personal information, and see how the other person responds. Keep in mind that self-disclosure is best in small doses. Over self-disclosing makes others uncomfortable.

17. **When you're concerned that what you have to say may be misunderstood:**
   a. Determine what your main message is In other words, don't get lost in the details. Can you say what you have to say in 30 seconds?
   b. Consider why it's important that you communicate this message to these particular people. In other words, clarify your intention: are you simply trying to express your ideas or are you trying to influence what they think?
   c. Say what you have to say as clearly and as succinctly as possible.

d. Check for understanding to ensure that others have understood your message as it was intended.

18. **Keep in mind that not everything that others say is interesting to us, BUT it may be interesting to them.** Likewise, something that interests us may be boring to others. Being attentive and respectful while others are talking is part of the give-and-take in relationships. Try to find something interesting in what others say by relating it to yourself, OR be interested simply because this other person is important to you.

19. When you're feeling shy about talking with people, **ask yourself, "What's the worst thing that could happen?"** Psychologist Jennice Vilhauer suggests that you tell yourself that your interaction will go well. Take every opportunity you get to talk with people. Be curious about other people.

BUILDING RELATIONSHIPS AT WORK

Don't let your hesitation get the best of you: the more practice you get in social situations, the more comfortable you will feel. Realize that others may be feeling shy, as well.

20. **Engage in *rewarding* communication behaviors**. According to Karl Albrecht's classic book, *Stress and the Manager*, these include:
   a. Giving others a chance to express views or share information
   b. Hearing the other person out
   c. Sharing yourself with others; smiling; greeting others
   d. Giving positive nonverbal messages of acceptance and respect
   e. Praising and complimenting others
   f. Expressing respect for others' values and opinions
   g. Giving suggestions constructively
   h. Talking positively and constructively
   i. Affirming others' feelings and needs

j. Treating others as equals
k. Delaying automatic reactions; not flying off the handle
l. Leveling with others

21. **Avoid high stress *punishing* behaviors.** Here are few examples from Albrecht:
    a. Using non-verbal put-downs
    b. Insulting or belittling someone
    c. Insisting that you get your own way
    d. Being negative or complaining
    e. Talking down to others
    f. Being dogmatic in expressing your opinions; "you're absolutely right, and others are wrong"
    g. Routinely disagreeing with others
    h. Showing frustration or simply checking out of a conversation
    i. Diverting the conversation on a whim
    j. Trying to make others feel guilty
    k. Being overly reactive and sensitive to what someone has said
    l. Focusing on yourself and your needs

22. **Don't expect others to read your mind.** Sometimes, we fall into the trap of thinking that others should automatically know what we want. However, regardless of how well they know us or what we consider to be conventional norms of etiquette, we need to express our needs and expectations directly. So, for example, if you want your partner to take initiative in organizing a date night, share your expectation with your partner along with a handful of ideas of things you might like to do.

23. **Influence others through your actions.** In his book *Principle-Centered Leadership*, management expert Stephen Covey offers several suggestions for influencing others, including:
    a. Not saying negative things
    b. Exercising self-restraint, especially when you or others are tired or emotions are frayed

BUILDING RELATIONSHIPS AT WORK

c. Putting things in perspective; asking what matters most
d. Thinking before reacting
e. Admitting your mistakes
f. Being patient with others, especially when you or others are stressed
g. Assuming the best of others; giving people the benefit of the doubt
h. Trying to understand what others are telling you before attempting to be understood
i. Taking the initiative to improve strained relationships
j. Allowing others to influence you; not being closed to others' opinions
k. Doing a service or favor in an anonymous manner
l. Being proactive; making conscious choices regarding how to act in a situation
m. Not being drawn into petty accusations

BUILDING RELATIONSHIPS AT WORK

n. Working through problems rather than avoiding them or fighting

o. Not shielding people from their irresponsible behavior

24. **Demonstrate respect for others.** In his article, *Vice and Virtue in Everyday Life*, ethics professor Douglas Chismar argues that our day-to-day civilities are a broader reflection of the quality of our character. He recommends some basic rules of etiquette:

a. Keep appointments and be punctual; don't make others wait for you to show up or be ready

b. Maintain good records for those who will follow in your position after you

c. Read your emails and return calls promptly

d. Return what you borrow (pens, files, catalogues)

e. Follow an agenda when you lead a meeting

BUILDING RELATIONSHIPS AT WORK

    f. Refill the coffee pot, the copy machine, and gas tank of the company car

    g. Share the spotlight: give recognition to others for their ideas and work; don't use others' ideas without giving credit

    h. Exercise patience with others who may be having a bad day

    i. Take the blame for mistakes you've made, instead of shifting the blame or demonizing others

    j. Don't use threats, pressure and coercion to get the job done

    k. Don't find entertainment in others' conflicts

    l. Don't scold or reprimand someone in front of others

25. **Improve communications with your boss.** Here are some tips offered by communication experts Clare Sproston and Glenna Sutcliffe in *20 Training Workshops for Listening Skills*.

BUILDING RELATIONSHIPS AT WORK

a. Postponing a discussion if it's a bad time
b. Not accosting your boss just before lunch
c. Avoiding times when your boss is tired or especially busy
d. Talking in terms of benefits to your boss and the organization
e. Getting straight to the point
f. Asking open questions
g. Using facts rather than vague feelings to back up your case
i. Talking about positives as well as negatives
j. Offering solutions and suggestions, rather than simply raising issues
k. Following up your discussion with a written summary that indicates who will do what by when

26. **Communicate effectively with your employees.** Sproston and Sutcliffe suggest the following:
   a. Having frequent informal meetings with them, so that you're up-to-date regarding their activities, and they're comfortable approaching you
   b. Giving them time to say what they have to say without being interrupted
   c. Avoiding distractions during your meetings. Not looking at your watch, cell phone, or computer when they're talking to you
   c. Listening to all of them equally, rather than paying attention mainly to your "favorites"
   d. Soliciting and being open to their suggestions for how to make things better
   e. Focusing on solutions, rather than meting out blame. Accepting blame when appropriate

f. Sharing information that will help them understand the organization and do their work

e. Making sure that the environment is private and uninterrupted

f. Checking your understanding by summarizing

g. Following through on commitments or agreements that you make

Develop effective messages.

McKay, Davis, and Fanning consider effective messages to be core communication skills. Here are some of their recommendations for expressing yourself effectively:

27. **Communicate your thoughts directly.** Don't simply assume that others know what you're thinking or feeling. And don't expect others to pick up on you hints or other indirect forms of communication.

28. **Express your thoughts in a timely fashion**; i.e., when they're relevant, and when others can see a connection between your observations and their behavior. Don't store your opinions, and then dump them in one load onto others.

29. **Express your needs and thoughts openly.** Communicate your purpose clearly and openly. Don't ask questions when you want to make a statement. Don't contradict yourself. Don't couch what you have to say in criticisms, compliments, or extraneous comments.

30. **Avoid things that cause others to be defensive:**
    a. Labelling others as stupid, selfish, evil, lazy, etc.
    b. Being sarcastic
    c. Dragging the past into conversations
    d. Making comparisons with others

e. Making accusations by using "You" messages; for example, "You never help out"

31. **Avoid hidden messages**, for example:
    a. I'm good (i.e., you're the hero of all your stories)
    b. I'm good (but you're not) (i.e., implied criticism)
    c. You're good (but I'm not) (i.e., flattery)
    d. I'm helpless, I suffer (i.e., victim role)
    e. I'm blameless (i.e., excuses for failures)
    f. I'm fragile (i.e., needing protection)
    g. I'm tough (i.e., superhero)
    h. I know it all (i.e., perpetual instructor)

Give effective feedback.

32. **Choose an appropriate time.** Although feedback is most useful right after the behavior or error occurred, keep the following in mind:

a. Give feedback right after the behavior occurred. Criticizing someone for the first time during a performance review for something done four months ago is likely to be met with a hazy memory and resentment.
b. Give feedback when you can be objective about the issue (not when you're angry, etc.).
c. Give feedback when the receiver seems ready to accept it. If they're upset, wait till they have calmed down.

33. **Provide feedback with care and courtesy.** Show that you care about the person, and that your intention is to help. You need to let the person know that you value them, even though they make mistakes from time to time.

34. **Provide descriptive rather than evaluative feedback.** Focus on problem behaviors, not the person's worth. Describe observable

actions rather than interpreting the actions (e.g., "You're checking your cellphone while I'm talking to you," NOT "You're tuned out." Focus on specific behaviors that the person can do something about, rather than making general statements (e.g., "You insisted that your opinion was correct," NOT "You dominated the conversation.").

35. **Let the person know what they did well.** Rarely is someone's behavior 100% negative.

36. **Ask the person to paraphrase what you've said to ensure that they understood what you said.**

BUILDING RELATIONSHIPS AT WORK

Receive feedback effectively.

37. **Avoid being defensive and overreacting.** Listen calmly to everything the person is saying, perhaps taking notes of the key points.

38. **Ask for specific examples and evidence that supports what the person is saying.** Consider the merits of what the person is saying. Realize that they may have incomplete or biased information.

39. **Agree with what you can agree with.** Offer your perspective without becoming argumentative or defensive. Offer facts and specific examples that support your point of view.

40. **Offer a meaningful response to any offers of help or suggestions.** Focus on improvements that are needed "going

forward," whether it's your behavior or how you communicate with each other.

Avoid communication difficulties.

41. **Avoid coming across as apathetic.** According to psychologist Robert Bolton, this happens when you're detached, and you show no emotions when interacting with others. Essentially, you're telling the person that you don't care. In contrast, empathy suggests that you understand and accept what the other person is saying and feeling. An example is, "Sounds like you're having a rough day." Bolton says that we need to separate empathy from sympathy. When we're sympathetic, we're overinvolved and feeling "for" another person rather than "with" them. An example is, "I feel horrible for you!"

BUILDING RELATIONSHIPS AT WORK

42. **Avoid people who gossip.** As missionary Lawrence Lovasik tells us in his book, *The Hidden Power of Kindness*, the gossip may give you the impression that you're a "favored one to whom they confide their information, but when you turn your back, you may be their victim."

43. **Avoid the following habits that fuel anger:**
    a. Not giving someone a chance to talk
    b. Interrupting while someone else is talking
    c. Not looking at the other person when they talk
    d. Acting bored or like the conversation is wasting your time
    e. Pacing and showing impatience
    f. Being sarcastic
    g. Finishing someone's story
    h. Twisting others' words or rephrasing what was said in a negative way

44. **Sidestep the barriers to communication.** Here's a sampling of the roadblocks identified by psychologist Thomas Gordon in his classic book, *Leader Effectiveness Training*.
    a. **Ordering, Commanding,** such as, "You must..." "You have to..." This results in resistance and rebellious behavior.
    b. **Warning, Threatening,** such as, "If you don't, then..." "You'd better, or..." This produces fear and resentment.
    c. **Advising, Giving Solutions**, such as, "Why don't you..." "Let me suggest..." This prevents people from thinking through problems on their own, and it suggests that others aren't able to solve their own problems.
    d. **Judging, Blaming**, such as, "You're not thinking maturely..." "You're lazy..." This criticism discourages others from communicating with you out of fear of negative judgment.

e. **Name-Calling, Ridiculing**, such as "What's that pimple between your ears?" This damages a person's self-esteem and causes defensiveness.

f. **Analyzing, Diagnosing**; such as, "What's wrong with you is..." "You don't really mean that." This results in anger, frustration, or a feeling of being talked down to.

g. **Diverting, Withdrawing**; such as, "Let's talk about something else," or remaining silent. The result is that issues aren't dealt with, and others feel that it's useless to bring issues to you.

45. **Before saying something negative to someone, consider psychologist Sidney Simon's filters for negative criticism:**
    a. Are they able to accept my criticism right now? If they're having a hard day, feeling drained, or dealing with major issues, they're not open to your criticism. It may be the last straw.

BUILDING RELATIONSHIPS AT WORK

b. Are you willing to work through the criticism or issue with the person? If you`re planning to simply "dump and run," your criticism won't do any good.

c. Has this person heard this criticism before? Often? If so, then you may be nagging the person. Rather than considering your criticism impartially, the person will feel harassed.

d. Is there something that this person can do to address the issue or improve the situation? If this person feels helpless and their hands are tied in some way, criticism won't have a positive effect.

e. Do you have any fears, shortcomings, or faults that are driving your criticism? In other words, is your criticism more about you than the other person? If so, you may want to examine "the log in your eye," before pointing out the sliver in someone else's eye.

f. Will criticism motivate this person to change? Building on someone`s strengths, rather than emphasizing their faults, is more likely to result in positive change in the future.

Build Positive Relationships

46. **Build your social network with a variety of people.** Volunteer to participate on cross-organizational committees and task forces. Demonstrate respect for influential people and appreciation for their wisdom, experience, and accomplishments.

47. **Support your manager in achieving goals.** Don't contradict or argue with your manager in public (e.g., in a meeting). Unless absolutely necessary, don't bypass your manager, and take a problem to your manager's boss. Try to resolve difficulties with your manager directly and in private. If your opinion differs from that of your manager, unless the issue pertains to ethics or legalities or is a matter of life and

BUILDING RELATIONSHIPS AT WORK

death, you may need to defer to your manager's opinion.

48. **Serve as a resource to others.** Become knowledgeable about issues, events, and developments beyond the boundaries of your job. Frame your opinions and ideas in terms of how they support organizational objectives.

49. **Remain calm when under pressure.** Demonstrate an ability to think through issues clearly and solve problems in a rational and politically sensitive manner.

50. **Build constructive relationships with coworkers.** Show an interest in other people as individuals and in their work. Look for shared interests. When asked to provide your opinion by coworkers, offer honest but tactful feedback. Don't belittle someone who has a lower level job.

BUILDING RELATIONSHIPS AT WORK

51. **Do favors for others, and allow them to help you out as well.** Don't be a lone ranger who doesn't accept help from others.

52. **Ask your manager and coworkers for work-related advice.** This shows that you value their opinions and trust their judgment. This option must be pursued in moderation, however, lest you be viewed as a pest or, worse, an incompetent person.

53. **Avoid being openly disloyal to your organization** by, for example, criticizing the organization or your manager in public.

BUILDING RELATIONSHIPS AT WORK

Be assertive.

54. **Avoid being passive or aggressive (or both) in your interactions with others.** According to psychologist Allan Hedberg, being passive leaves you feeling exploited, resentful, and helpless. Being aggressive destroys your relationships and credibility with others. Being assertive is the better choice: respecting your rights and those of others. Here are a few insights that Hedberg offers in this regard:

   a. You gain self-respect and respect from others when you stand up for yourself and express your thoughts directly and appropriately.

   b. If you want others to share their thoughts and feelings with you, you must do the same.

   c. By telling people how their behavior is affecting you, you give them a chance to change their behavior.

BUILDING RELATIONSHIPS AT WORK

After reading these tips, review the ones that you have circled, checked, or highlighted. What do they have in common?

4

DILEMMAS: WHAT WOULD YOU DO?

This section gives you the opportunity to consider how to apply what you've just learned. Read all of the following situations, and answer the reflection questions in your learning journal. Then, explain why you answered the way you did and how you might apply this at work.

BUILDING RELATIONSHIPS AT WORK

Bob the Hard Worker

Bob came from a working class background where he learned that he needed to work hard to get ahead. His father often told him, "If you work hard, your boss will notice you, and you'll get ahead." So, Bob is as diligent as possible; he follows his supervisor's instructions and does his work on time and in a quality manner. He's cordial to others, but doesn't engage in small talk or extend a helping hand. This would take time away from work. He doesn't bother going to social events or even lunch with others. He works at his desk during lunch time, and he leaves promptly at the end of the work day. At team meetings, he listens and nods in support of his supervisor's proposed changes, but he doesn't recommend any changes himself, despite seeing some opportunities for improvement. Once he's the supervisor, he'll initiate changes (not just implement them). He thinks that Breana is an apple polisher who avoids work, and Bailey is a pain in the –.

BUILDING RELATIONSHIPS AT WORK

Breana the Schmoozer

Breana likes talking with people. She learned that the best way to get ahead in life was to get along well with others. She performs her duties at acceptable levels. It's clear, however, that she isn't as hard working, smart, or technically competent as Bob. Where she really shines is by helping to smooth relationships between people. When she hears that one person has a problem, she connects them with another person who can solve the problem. She's in touch with what's going on in the organization. Like Bailey, she sees room for improvement in the organization. But, instead of complaining, she recommends or suggests changes at team meetings. Before doing so, she "tests the waters" with her boss and some influential colleagues: she talks to them about her suggestions, gets their ideas, and modifies her ideas before presenting them at a meeting. She organizes team social events and plays badminton with senior managers.

BUILDING RELATIONSHIPS AT WORK

Bailey the Complainer

Bailey does the minimum necessary to get by. If you ask Bailey why he isn't more productive, he will get defensive, "How dare you say that? You try doing my job with the limited resources that I have. I don't see YOU taking work home!" And he will huff and puff and walk away before you could respond. At coffee break, if people talk about their challenges, he joins in and talks about his problems nonstop to anyone within ear shot. But, also, he tries to solve their problems for them. He tells them that they're stupid and making mistakes, and that they need to follow his advice. One piece of advice he gives frequently is that they should harass the boss for more resources (after all the squeaky wheel gets the grease). That's what he does. Bailey thinks that he could do a better job of running the place than his boss, and he often tells his boss and his coworkers this.

BUILDING RELATIONSHIPS AT WORK

Reflection Questions

1. Using the ideas presented in this book, how would you describe Bob, Breana, and Bailey's ability to communicate and build relationships?
2. Their current manager is being promoted. Who would you choose to fill the manager's position? Why?
3. What advice would you give to Bob, Breana and Bailey to improve their communication and relationship building skills?
4. How could these actions and strategies apply to your staff and workplace?

5
PLANNING FOR ACTION

Complete the following planning exercises in your learning journal.

BUILDING RELATIONSHIPS AT WORK

Part A: Communication Situations

Describe as specifically as possible three interpersonal interactions that you will face in the next month and that you feel anxious about. These could include problems with your boss, coworker, employee, or someone else. Don't use situations where you're providing feedback to someone else; save those for Part B. For each situation:
1. Describe the situation briefly.
2. Prepare a script that demonstrates that you're being respectful of your own needs and those of others.

(Inspired by Paddy O'Brien's *Positive Management: Assertiveness for Managers*.)

BUILDING RELATIONSHIPS AT WORK

Part B: Feedback Planning

Think of a situation in which you feel anxious about giving feedback to someone.
1. Describe the situation.
2. Describe what is causing you to feel anxious about the situation.
3. Plan what you will say to the other person.
4. Explain why it's important that you give this feedback (i.e. what's in it for you and for the person receiving the feedback).
5. Identify where and when you will give this feedback.

If possible, practice this feedback session with a friend playing the role of the person receiving the feedback.

About the Managerial Competencies Series

What's in the series?

This series is built around four managerial competency clusters: personal, people, purpose, and process.

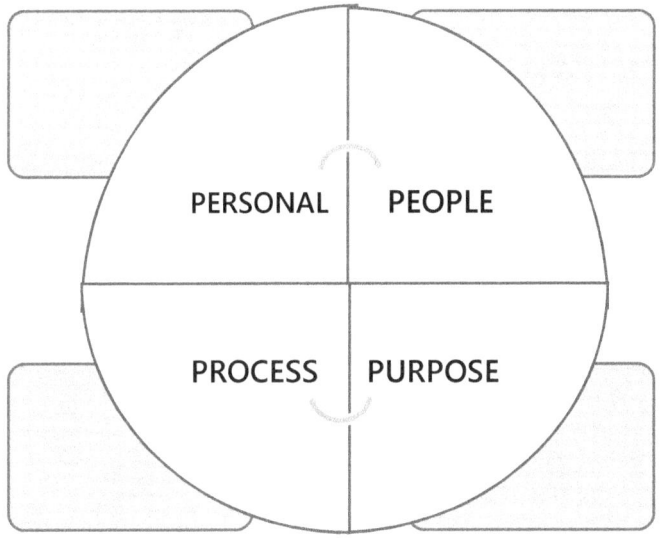

Each cluster is made up of several competencies possessed by awesome managers. The series addresses a total of 15 competencies, each of which is the topic of a book of around 100 pages. Let's look at each cluster one at a time.

Personal Competencies

The starting point of the series is developing personal skills, given that effective self-management is essential for managing people, programs, and processes. It goes without saying that to manage others, you first must be able to manage yourself. People who are familiar with their personal strengths and challenges and who engage in effective self-management tend to work well with others.

BUILDING RELATIONSHIPS AT WORK

Here are the competencies included in the Personal Competencies cluster:

1. **Living the Core Values**, which involves demonstrating honesty, truthfulness, trustworthiness, reliability, fairness, and ethicality in all your decisions and interactions.
2. **Developing Personal Mastery** through personal responsibility, emotional resilience, constructive attitudes, self-confidence, adaptability, conscientiousness, and competence.
3. **Organizing Yourself** by focusing on your

BUILDING RELATIONSHIPS AT WORK

priorities and making effective use of time.
4. **Building Stress Resilience**, which deals with managing life's stresses by developing personal hardiness.

People Competencies

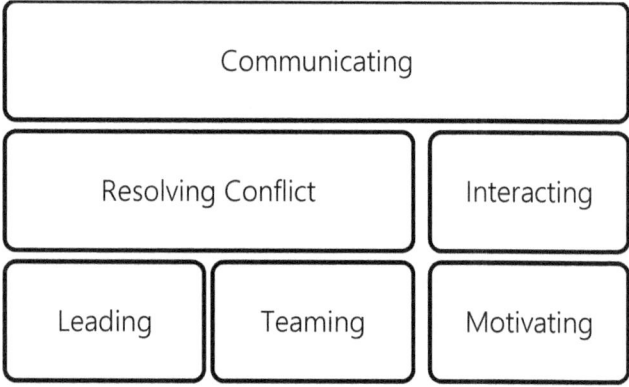

This cluster helps you examine and build your skills in working with and managing others. Although it's important for managers to be *technically* competent in order to gain credibility, interpersonal skills make the difference between awesome and not-so-awesome managers.

BUILDING RELATIONSHIPS AT WORK

The competencies included in the People Competencies cluster are:

5. **Communicating in Writing and through Presentations**, which focuses on communicating ideas effectively, whether verbally or in writing.
6. **Creating Employee Engagement**, creating motivating working conditions so that staff contribute their best to the organization.
7. **Building Relationships**, which considers how to interact with others through effective listening and responding.
8. **Resolving Conflict**, which addresses how to deal with conflict in a productive manner.
9. **Leading Your Team**, which means leading in a manner that is appropriate for the needs of the situation and your team.
10. **Cultivating Team Spirit** by building a cohesive, high-performing team.

BUILDING RELATIONSHIPS AT WORK

Purpose and Process Competencies

This final cluster combines two sets of competencies. Purpose competencies offer you a "big picture" perspective of your organization and your own role in the organization. Process competencies help you translate this "big picture" (the *whats*) into everyday practice (the *hows*). In other words, they allow you to consider how work should be done as a means of accomplishing the goals of your organization and your work unit.

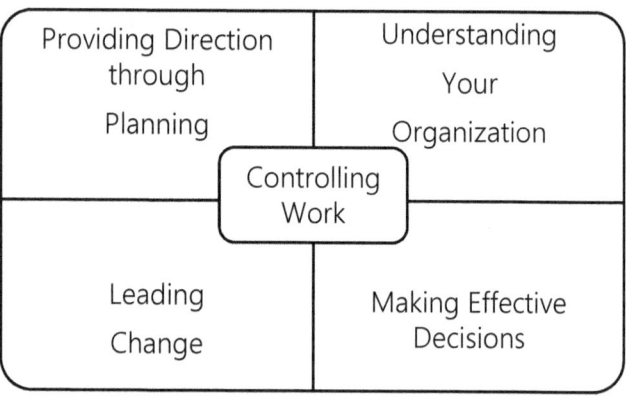

BUILDING RELATIONSHIPS AT WORK

Purpose and Process competencies include:

11. **Making Effective Decisions**, whether individually or in a team setting.
12. **Controlling Work Performance** by establishing control mechanisms to ensure results.
13. **Providing Direction through Planning**, which discusses the management process and offers tips for setting organizational direction and developing operational plans that fit this direction.
14. **Understanding Your Organization**, in other words, understanding the principles of organizing work and creating the right structure for your work unit.
15. **Leading Change** so that your organization and team thrive.

How is each book organized?

Each book is organized according to a five-step learning process. This process is designed to help you learn in an active and reflective manner.

In each book, after a brief introduction, we jump right into the "**reality check**." This series of self-coaching questions is meant to help you reflect on and develop insight into your own strengths and weaknesses in relation to a particular competence and, hopefully, motivate you to work on building your competencies.

The reality check consists of the kinds of questions that management coaches might ask you, but that you can simply ask yourself. Just be sure to give yourself a chance to answer them!

Management coaches help managers view and understand situations from a variety of perspectives. But, if the art of coaching is asking challenging questions (as management coach Chantal Binet says), why not ask yourself these questions?

Second, to accompany you on your learning journey, you're offered a curated collection of **inspirational quotes**. There's lots of wisdom available from people from all walks of life. The quotes that grab us and speak to us do so because they have touched a nerve in us. They resonate with us, perhaps because they offer a message that we need to hear to continue developing or because they challenge us to become better people.

Third, we offer you tons of **tips and tricks** of awesome managers. These practical tips cover a gamut of perspectives and actions that you can take to improve your competencies. Ideally, they will encourage you to consider the variety of possibilities and alternatives that are available to you. It's up to you to decide which are the most useful to you. As you read this section, be sure to note or highlight the tips that stand out for you.

Next, we present a series of **dilemmas** or situations for you to resolve. This section will help you see how you might apply the tips and tricks from the previous section. We ask you to read the situation and then identify what you would do in these situations. You might choose one of the alternatives that is offered, or you might come up with your own creative solution. Ultimately, there are many factors and perspectives that might influence what is the "best" choice.

Finally, we nudge you to develop an **action plan** that you will *actually* implement.

BUILDING RELATIONSHIPS AT WORK

Developing and implementing an action plan is an especially important step because it helps you draw value from your efforts in working through this series. After all, you're reading this book because you're hoping to become an awesome manager, right? This means developing a realistic plan that describes the actions that you intend to take to become an awesome manager, implementing your plan, reflecting on how well it worked, and then continuously making any adjustments that are needed. So, the cycle starts again!

How can you get the most out of the series?

You can read one or two books per month for an entire year, creating and implementing action plans for each book. Ultimately, this will help you develop a better understanding of yourself as a manager, your expectations, your strengths, and your areas for improvement.

As a way of refreshing your competencies, you can even re-read the books and re-visit your action plans in the future. Depending on what's happening in your life (new job, new team, new challenges), every time you read these books, you may develop new insights that help you deal with a situation.

BUILDING RELATIONSHIPS AT WORK

The knowledge of the world is only to be acquired in the world, and not in a closet.
Lord Chesterfield

What we have to learn to do,
we learn by doing.
Aristotle

Life is a succession of lessons which must be lived to be understood.
Ralph Waldo Emerson

What do this British statesman from the 1600s, Greek philosopher from 384 B.C., and American poet from the 1800s have in common? They all agree that learning comes from trying new things, not from simply sitting back and reading a book.

Don't just read the books; *do* them! Just reading the books won't transform you into an awesome manager. If you just read the books, you might get to know a lot about what it means to be an awesome manager without changing what you do in the workplace. How useful is that? Just like learning to ride a bike, it's impossible to develop your skills by simply reading or even thinking about what you have read. Besides, as *The Matrix* reminds us, "There's a difference between knowing the path and walking it."

In order to truly learn from our experiences, we need to do a complete loop of the learning cycle: we need to reflect on our experiences, figure out what lessons we learned, consider ways to apply these lessons, and then apply them. You may know people who seem to repeat the same mistakes over and over again or people who continually approach situations in a manner that doesn't work for them. It's probably because they go through life without taking the time to reflect, consider what they've learned, and develop an action plan in order to change their experiences. They're stuck somewhere on the learning cycle. David Kolb, the creator of this learning cycle, says that we all have a favorite place on the cycle where we tend to get stuck.

Some people simply enjoy reading the books and reflecting on how they may relate to their lives, hopefully finding an opportunity to make use of their learning at some point in the future. However, without specific goals and action plans, they're not extracting as much value as they could from their investment of time and money.

Although this is partly due to differences in learning styles, it's also due to a reluctance to try something new and different. This may be caused by a fear of stepping out of one's comfort zone: what is familiar is comfortable. It may also be caused by a desire to accumulate a truckload of knowledge or have the perfect circumstances, such as the ideal boss or set of employees, before acting. Some of us think and think and continue to think without taking action. That used to be my personal downfall until I realized that knowing lots about a topic isn't the same as learning or making a difference in real life!

At the other extreme, some of us take action without first reflecting on our experiences and what we learned from them. Some people prefer to go ahead and try things out right away. They're more action-oriented than their reflective counterparts. These folks typically find it especially challenging to slow down, consciously reflect on what they're reading, and develop a well thought out action plan before acting. In the same way, if you just read the books and do nothing else, the learning process will get stuck right off the bat.

Reflecting and taking action is the best solution. It's not enough to *know* how to do something. Although it's helpful and important to take the time to reflect and develop insights, at some point, you need to *do* the work yourself. Otherwise, as management expert Peter Block has said, "Waiting becomes an excuse for not acting."

Here are **five other important things** to do to maximize your learning. First, **keep a learning journal**. Record your thoughts as you read the books, answer the self-coaching questions, and develop your action plans. It will help you clarify your thinking, see patterns in what you have been experiencing and writing, and serve as a record of commitments you have made to yourself through your action plans. You'll be able to look back at what you've written and be impressed with all that you've learned! You could use a notebook or create an electronic document. Some people even email journal entries to themselves as a way of recording the day and time of their entries.

Second, **pull together a feedback team** who can help you get the most from this series. Your feedback team could be a group of four or five people that you have confidence in, such as coworkers, your manager, friends, and family members. Don't be shy about asking people for their support in helping you become a better manager; they are more willing to help you than you might think! These discussions will offer you different perspectives and exponentially increase how much you learn from the series. Besides, awesome managers surround themselves with people they trust who are willing to give them honest feedback that will help them grow as individuals.

In supporting you, others can play one or more of the following roles:

→ The Head: These people can help you analyze a question or problem objectively. They can sketch out options, compare data, or simply provide you with accurate information.

→ The Heart: These people can help you express your emotions and understand them better. They listen, cheer you up, don't make judgments, and give you a sense of security.

→ The Legs/Arms: These people help you do things. They go places with you; they make you get moving when you don't feel like it. These people energize you.

BUILDING RELATIONSHIPS AT WORK

How can your manager help? Can your manager provide feedback, advice and tips, and time to complete the series? What will you do to get your manager's help? For example, could you meet with your manager once every two weeks to discuss your progress and talk about how to manage effectively?

How can your peers help? Can your peers provide feedback, tips about managing, or coaching when needed? What will you do to get their help? Could you schedule a coffee break with them once every two weeks to discuss what you're learning and to share tips? Can you work through the series together?

How can your employees help? Can your employees provide feedback regarding your strengths and opportunities for improvement or work with you to develop a plan for making your unit function more effectively? What will you do to get their help? Could you meet with them once every two weeks to discuss what you're learning and how your team can implement elements of your action plan?

How can your friends help? Could they provide feedback, tips about managing, and encouragement for you to try new things? What will you do to get their help? Could you organize a dinner with them once every two weeks to discuss what you're learning and how to implement your action plan?

Third, **develop and implement a SMARTER action plan.** You know you've really learned something when your behavior changes (for the better, of course). Insights and tips that are meaningful to you will change your perspective *and* your behaviors. That's why each book ends by inviting you to develop an action plan. Your plan should be **Specific, Measurable, Attainable, Realistic, Timely, Exciting, and Rewarded.** Think about things that you need to start doing, stop doing, or

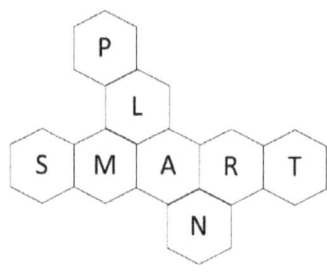

continue doing. Here's an example: "By the end of next week, I will write two letters – one to my former manager and one to my best friend – expressing my gratitude for their coaching and willingness to challenge me to become a better person. I will send these letters by email no later than Friday afternoon." Write your action plan in your journal. Revisit it to check your progress, and revise your plan as needed. Remember to ask for help from others, evaluate your progress, and reward yourself for your progress toward becoming an awesome manager.

Fourth, **identify obstacles or barriers that might get in your way of making the most of the series** and implementing your action plans; for example, lack of time or energy, poor personal habits, others' expectations, etc. List these in the column labelled "Obstacles" on the following page. Now, think about specific actions that you can take to address them and place these in the "Neutralizers" column; for example, meet with your manager, plan small

BUILDING RELATIONSHIPS AT WORK

wins or ways to celebrate your progress, etc.

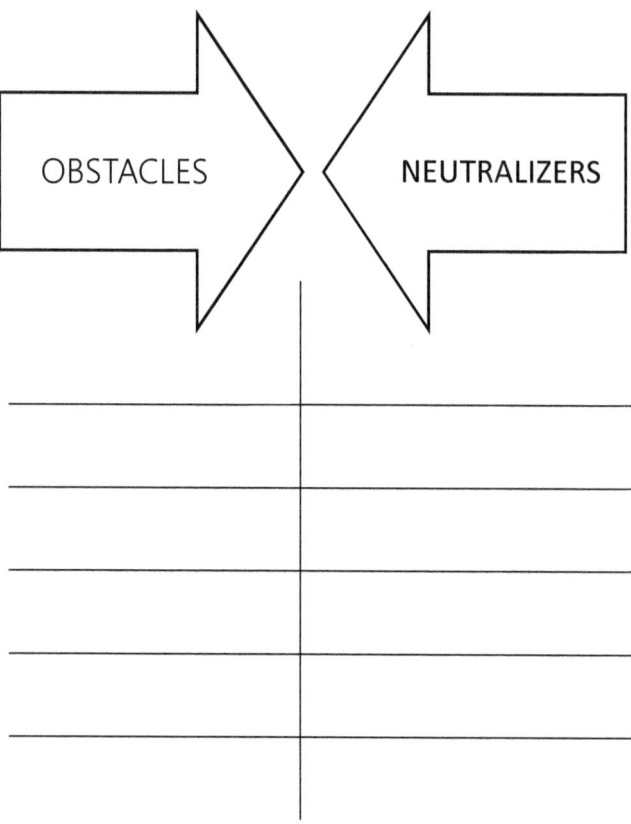

BUILDING RELATIONSHIPS AT WORK

Finally, do what you need to do to motivate yourself. Don't wait to be motivated to get started. Instead, get started, and motivation will come knocking at your door!

Also, try to be comfortable with discomfort. As you change how you manage, you may meet with some resistance from those around you. You exist in a system of relationships. Because systems are geared toward equilibrium (stability), if you change one thing in the system, the equilibrium is shot, and the system is upset. There may be pressure from others and from your own sense of comfort for you to do what you've always done regardless of whether or not it works.

It may be tempting to give up when things feel unnatural, but rest assured that this is part of the learning process. It's normal that trying out new ways of doing things makes you feel a bit uncomfortable in one way or another. Sometimes, we come across awesome folks who do their work without hesitation and seemingly without effort. It's easy to forget that they've gone through the highs and lows of the learning process. For example, think of Cirque du Soleil acrobats who seem to perform stunts with ease and pinpoint accuracy. It took them lots of practice, repetition, and even occasional failures to get to that skill level. Experts make things look easy.

Are you ready to begin your awesome journey? Earl Nightingale once said, "All you need is the plan, the road map, and the courage to press on to your destination." I hope that this series serves as your guide and road map on your journey toward awesomeness.

REFERENCES

Adler, R.B., & Towne, N. (1993). *Looking out/looking in* (7th Ed.). Fort Worth, TX: Harcourt Brace College Publishers.

Albrecht, K. (1986). *Stress and the manager*. Touchstone.

Beebe, S., Beebe, S., & Redmond, M. (2016). *Interpersonal communication: Relating to others* (8h Ed.). Pearson Education Canada.

Bolton, R. (1979). *People skills: How to assert yourself, listen to others, and resolve conflicts*. New York: Simon & Schuster.

Bienvenu, M. (1974). Interpersonal communication skills inventory. In J.W. Pfeiffer & J.E. Jones (Eds.). The 1974 annual handbook for group facilitators; San Diego CA: University Associates.

Cawood, D. (1983). *Assertiveness for managers*. Vancouver: Self-Counsel Press.

Chartier, M. (1974). The 1974 Annual Handbook for Group Facilitation. La Jolla, CA: University Associates.

Chismar, D. (2001). Vice and virtue in everyday life. *Journal of Business Ethics*, 29, 169-186.

Covey, S. (1991). *Principle-centered leadership*. New York: Simon & Schuster.

DuBrin, A. J. (1994) Sex differences in the use and effectiveness of tactics of impression management. Psychological Reports, 74, 531-544.

Folger, R. & Cropanzano, R. (1998). *Organizational justice and human resource management*. SAGE.

Gordon, T. (2001). *Leader effectiveness training: LET (Revised):" LET"*. Penguin.

Hedberg, A. (2012). Achieving and Living a Healthy Lifestyle in a World of Stress: 70 Lessons for Those Wanting Improved Health and Lower Health Care Costs. AuthorHouse.

Lanier, K., The Christian Science Monitor. (1998). A chatting pro proves small talk is no big deal. From: https://www.csmonitor.com/1998/1124/112498.feat.feat.6.html

Lovasik, L. (1999). *The hidden power of kindness*. Manchester, NH: Sophia Institute Press.

McKay, M., Davis, M., & Fanning, P. (2018). *Messages: The communication skills book*. (4th ed.) Oakland: New Harbinger Publications.

O'Brien, P. (1994). *Positive management: Assertiveness for managers*. San Diego: Pfeiffer.

Simon, S. (1979). Negative criticism: and what you can do about it. Values Press.

Seitz, V. A. (2001). *Your executive image: How to look your best & project success for men and women*. Adams Media Corp.

Sproston, C. & Sutcliffe, G.E. (1989). *20 Training workshops for listening skills*.

Vilhauer, J., Psychology Today. (2016) 4 ways to overcome shyness. From: https://www.psychologytoday.com/us/blog/living-forward/201612/4-ways-overcome-shyness

BUILDING RELATIONSHIPS AT WORK

Playbooks in the Managerial Competencies Series

1. Living the Core Values
2. Developing Personal Mastery
3. Organizing Yourself
4. Building Stress Resilience
5. Communicating in Writing and Through Presentations
6. Creating Employee Engagement
7. Building Relationships at Work
8. Resolving Conflict
9. Leading Your Team
10. Cultivating Team Spirit
11. Making Effective Decisions
12. Controlling Work Performance
13. Providing Direction through Planning
14. Understanding Your Organization
15. Leading Change

www.ingramcontent.com/pod-product-compliance
Lightning Source LLC
Chambersburg PA
CBHW070304230526
45470CB00002B/709